Usborne

Little First Stickers

Tractors
and
Trucks

Illustrated by
Joaquin Camp

You'll find all the stickers at the back of the book.

Words by Hannah Watson
Designed by Kirsty Tizzard

Sowing seeds

Farmers drive tractors up and down their fields
to loosen the soil, so they can plant lots of seeds.
Fill the fields with busy tractors.

Stick on a milk
truck driving along
this road.

Find a barn to stick in this field.

At the market

Stallholders arrive in their trucks early each morning with fruit, flowers and fresh fish to sell at the market. Add lots of animals setting up their stalls.

CATH'S CAKES

FRESH FISH

Fill the market with delivery trucks.

ICE CREAM

5

In the town

Recycling trucks and street sweeper trucks keep this busy town in order. Find a place for each one on the roads, then add more vehicles to the scene.

Stick on a fire truck leaving the fire station.

BOOKS

Find a van to help
these animals move
to a new house.

Collecting crops

At harvest time, farmers use lots of big machines to collect their crops. Find a place for a blue combine harvester cutting down wheat.

Stick on a tractor trimming the hedge.

Add some tractors
hauling bales.

In the mountains

Mountain vehicles have big wheels that help them to grip on to rocky slopes. Find a place to stick a tractor clearing some rubble from the road.

Stick on a truck going through the tunnel.

Construction site

These workers are building new houses.
They need to mix concrete in big tanks and
pour it out to make strong foundations.

Stick on some dump trucks.

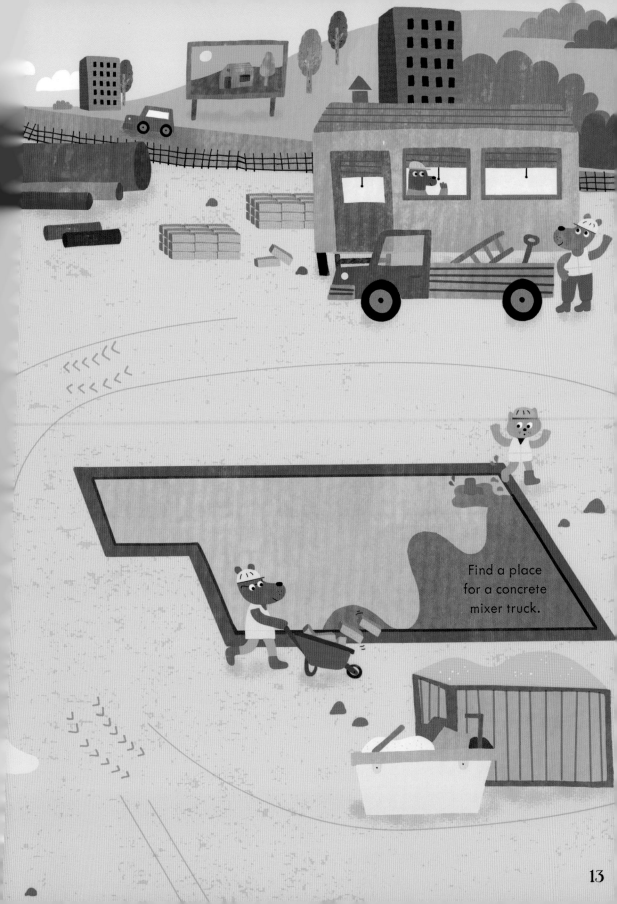

Find a place
for a concrete
mixer truck.

Monster trucks

Crowds cheer as the monster trucks at this
show perform daring jumps and flips. Fill the
arena with noisy trucks, then add cannons
letting off fireworks.

Add a truck
jumping over this ramp.

Stick on some more
firework cannons.

Workshop

Farmers bring their tractors to this workshop to have them fixed.
Fill the yard with workers repairing and cleaning the tractors,
to make them good as new.

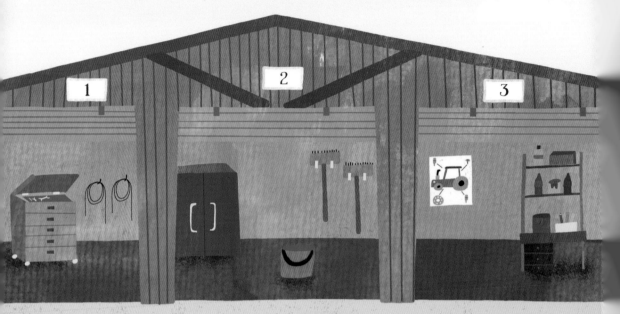

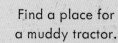

Find a place for
a muddy tractor.